STRENGTH

FOR THE WEARY

Finding Grace in Times of Trial

BY

NEW WAY TODAY

New Way Today

Published by Kathleen Hammer
ISBN-13: 978-1499667387
ISBN-10: 1499667388

Author website information:
www.newwaytoday.net
www.instagram.com/newwaytoday1

"Come to Me,
all you who are weary
and burdened,

and I will give you rest."

(Matthew 11:28)

New Way Today

Contents

New Way Today

Introduction

Your suffering has value. It's not nothing. Your struggle is not pointless, and it hasn't gone unnoticed by God. He sees it. He knows your heart. He knows your story. He knows your pain. He hears your prayers. He knows every tear and every fear. He knows that it doesn't make sense right now. He knows every step you take and how challenging it can be. He knows you're tired. He knows you completely and loves you immensely. You're not being punished.

Human suffering is a great mystery, but it has eternal value when we unite it to the cross of Christ. This may not feel like much of a comfort right now but as we surrender our struggles to Jesus, with faith and trust, we will receive the graces we need at this time in our lives, graces of inner strength and calm.

"Strength For The Weary, Finding Grace in Times of Trial," is a simple, practical and imperfect book with a sincere purpose - to build up the body of Christ and lift up the discouraged. To inspire us to look to Jesus as the source of our strength and peace, and to encourage one another to keep going in faith. God promises to refresh us and renew us. *"I will give you a new heart and put a new spirit in you"* (Ez 36:26). During difficult

7

times, we are called to believe and to trust that God will do what He says He will.

"For I know well the plans I have in mind for you," says the Lord. "They are plans for good and not for disaster, plans to give you a future full of hope" (Jer 29:11). God really does have a plan for our happiness. He not only has something better in mind, He has something wonderful in store. When we open our hearts to His plan, we will receive grace and be *"able to accomplish far more than all we ask or imagine, by the power at work within us"* (Eph 3:20).

We've been praying for help and help is on the way. In the meantime God has given us loving instruction. He has given us the answer we need for right now. We are to stick close to His Son, Jesus Christ, and follow Him.

Our Lord extends this invitation to each one of us in a new way today, *"Come to Me, all you who are weary and burdened, and I will give you rest"* (Mt 11:28). He opens His hand and extends it to us now, and asks us to take it. He calls upon us to trust in Him, to keep our eyes fixed on Him in the midst of the storm.

Sometimes, to our confusion, He asks for an amazing amount of this trust from us, more than we feel capable of. Nevertheless, the hand that is reaching out to us is where our strength, our hope, our rest and our peace will come from, and He will provide us even the grace to trust Him. He will give us everything we need to keep moving forward.

God is the source of all good. He is Goodness itself. God is Love, and Love loves us. We can safely place ourselves, and our loved ones, in His capable hands. We may have to let go of what is in ours, but as we learn to surrender and trust, grace will begin to flow, and overflow.

We don't carry our burdens alone. Jesus is by our side. He hasn't left us. We worship a risen Christ who is with us still, who gives us His Holy Spirit within us to be our strength. Our Heavenly Father doesn't abandon His children. He can't. He loves us too much. Our Creator cannot separate Himself from what He has made. God is within us, and "*He who is in you is greater than he who is in the world*" (1 John 4:4).

Suffering is a mystery, but it is also holy. We know this because Jesus Christ suffered. Jesus is God, so therefore God has suffered for us and understands our pain. It is when we look to the cross that we find our strength. Not from some disinterested and unapproachable God who could care less but from one who understands our need for strength, from someone who has suffered as well, from someone who also cried out to our Heavenly Father feeling abandoned by Him. In the mystery of our suffering, this is the person we look to for strength.

We cling to Jesus when things don't make sense and an amazing thing happens. We benefit from His suffering. We find strength to endure. He has won for us what we need. *"He was pierced for our offenses, crushed for our sins. Upon Him was the chastisement that makes us whole, by His stripes we were healed"* (Isaiah 53:5). It is through the wounds of Christ that we find healing for ourselves. Jesus has already purchased the graces we need. It is because of His death, that we can have a new life.

Our Lord understands we can't do it all. In fact, on our own strength we can't do anything. Without God we wouldn't even be able to take our next breath. We need our Creator. He is the source of our lives, and will be the source of our strength. The weary can find rest in Him because everything comes from Him. We can find the peace He promised us because He is the source of all peace. God is Love, and there is no other. He is a good God who, despite the struggles we are going through right now, remains good always.

In *"Strength For The Weary, Finding Grace in Times of Trial,"* I hope we will find encouragement and peace. I hope we will be able to breathe again, a new fresh breath of The Spirit, who will grace us with a new enthusiasm for life. This book is more of a message than anything else. We have a Savior, and He will help us.

Each chapter is composed of a scripture followed by a reflection and a prayer. It is similar in structure to New Way Today's book, *"A New You! Letting Go of the Past, Trusting God with our Future,"* which is another excellent spiritual resource. I pray that *"Strength For The Weary"* will refresh our souls and that through prayer, God's grace, and His word spoken to us through scripture, we will grow in faith and begin to trust Jesus more and more in our daily lives.

There is plenty out there to make us weary, but there is nothing in the world like what's inside of us to conquer it. We need to open our eyes of faith, and trust that the Creator of everything can fix anything. He will heal us and help us. He will uphold us, and even carry us, when we are feeling overwhelmed.

"But Jesus immediately said to them, 'Take courage! It is I. Don't be afraid.' 'Lord, if it's you,' Peter replied, 'tell me to come to you on the water.' 'Come,' He said. Then Peter got down out of the boat, walked on the water and came toward Jesus. But when he saw the wind, he was afraid and, beginning to sink, cried out, 'Lord, save me!' Immediately Jesus reached out his hand and caught him. 'You of little faith,' He said, 'why did you doubt?' And when they climbed into the boat, the wind died down. Then those who were in the boat worshiped Him, saying, 'Truly you are the Son of God'" (Matt 14:27-32).

God is here, now, ready to lift us up. Let's keep our eyes on Jesus, not on the storm. Let's loosen our grip and take His hand, which is always available. Hope begins here. Healing begins here. Strength comes from here. When we give God our hand and say *"Lord, save me!"* This is the first step we take in finding new strength, admitting we can't pull ourselves up. We need our God.

God Loves us so much. He Loves us at all times, in all circumstances and without conditions. His Love is the strength we need. May the Love, Grace, and Strength of God begin to flourish in our hearts, minds and souls in a New Way, Today.

1

He gives power to the weak, and strength to the powerless ... those who hope in the Lord will find new strength. They will soar high on wings like eagles. They will run and not grow weary. They will walk and not faint.

(Isaiah 40:29,31)

We can't do anything without God. We are completely dependent upon Him. We would not exist without Him. He is the source of our next breath and causes our hearts to beat. We have life because of Him.

God is *"the Alpha and the Omega, the First and the Last, the Beginning and the End"* (Rev 22:13) and we come from Him. So much turmoil within us would dissipate if we truly understood our place. We are the work of His hands, not the other way around. We belong to Him. He is, and He should be, in control. It's simply the natural order of things. God came first, we came second.

From this basic premise that we belong to God and from His revelation of Himself to us as

13

Love, we are called to live out our daily lives. Knowing our Creator Loves us is the true secret to happiness in life. Knowing who we are, a child of God, is where real strength comes from. Our Lord has told us, *"the truth will set you free"* (John 8:32). When we accept this truth and look at *who* we come from, we find ourselves receiving the power that comes from Him.

By faith, we open the floodgate of grace and activate God's power within us. Jesus said, *"Whoever believes in me, as Scripture has said, rivers of living water will flow from within them"* (John 7:38). We are connected to Christ and we can tap into the love and power of almighty God, who longs to give us *"every spiritual blessing"* (Eph 1:3).

When we are feeling weary we can go into prayer with this mindset, with a heart trusting and open like a child in need, and our Heavenly Father will not only lift us up but cause us to *"soar high on wings like eagles."* God will do far and above what we could ask or imagine. The important thing is to have confidence in God's Love for us, that He won't leave us feeling worn out. He hears our prayers, and *those who hope in the Lord will find new strength.*

Jesus walks with us every day. It's a very painful thing to feel alone, to be discouraged, to think no one cares, but our Lord wants us to know that He does care about every detail of our lives. He understands what's happening and He knows the graces we need to cope with our situation. He will provide us the strength to come through this trial better than before. Our Lord told us, "*I am with you always*" (Mt 28:20). He is with us now. Let's lay down our burden at His feet, and rest in Him.

"May the God of hope fill you with all joy and peace as you trust in Him, so that you may overflow with hope by the power of the Holy Spirit." (Romans 15:13)

Prayer

Dear Lord, you are all powerful and have promised to give power and strength to the weak. Lord, please pick me up and carry me through this time of my life, and don't let me go. I'm trying my best but it doesn't seem to be enough. Help me to realize and appreciate that you are close to me in this trial. Help me to learn what it is that you are trying to teach me. Help me not to be concerned with what others think, but only that I follow you in this matter. Help me to love others as you love me. Help me to rely on your strength, as mine continues to fail me. But I know that by your grace, all things can be made new.

Please give me a fresh outlook and a new hope. Please grant me the grace to trust you now even more than I ever have before. Please help me to be happy where you have placed me in life and to offer to you my daily tasks. Help me to be a faithful child of God, relying on you for everything I need. Help me to be at peace, knowing you are the one in charge. You have control over this situation and I ask you to keep me in peace as you work everything together for my good and renew me from the inside out.

I'll take those eagle's wings Lord. I thank you for them and for all the graces you give to me. Steer me in your direction. Open my heart and show me the way, and sustain me on the path to you. Guide me Lord, for in you is my strength. Bless, help, and heal me and my loved ones, and bring us into a new time of our lives, one where we are spiritually free, strong, and united in you. In Jesus name. Amen.

2

"I am the vine, you are the branches. If you remain in me and I in you, you will bear much fruit; apart from me you can do nothing"

(John 15:5)

Jesus didn't tell us this for the heck of it and He didn't tell us this to restrict us. *"I have told you this so that my joy may be in you and that your joy may be complete"* (John 15:11). God wants us to be happy, and He knows that the truth will set us free. Therefore He instructs us and teaches us, so that we can have this joy He promises.

The world can't give us this joy that Jesus refers to. It doesn't have the power. Jesus has the power. This lasting joy that we long for cannot be found apart from Him. He refers to it as *"my joy"* and makes it clear that He would like us to have it so that it can now be our joy too. It comes from Him and *the joy of the Lord is our strength* (Nehemiah 8:10).

God reveals Himself to us in scripture and Jesus is telling us the truth, that He is the source of

17

life and as long as we stay connected to Him, we will have life too. We need to *"remain in Him"* and stay united to the source of strength, from whom we will receive strength for ourselves.

"As the Father has loved me, so have I loved you. Now remain in my love" (John 15:9). Jesus loves us with the same exact love that The Father has for Him. It is the same Holy Spirit by which we are loved. Jesus is telling us that our Heavenly Father loves us and we can be united to The Father also, by remaining in Him.

It's an amazing thing to wake up each day with confidence saying, "My Father is God!" We can make a concrete decision to acknowledge our place, a branch united to The Vine, who loves us and has the power to give us the graces we need.

We all have a place in the Kingdom. We are all a part of God's plan in some way and each one of us is called to personal holiness, which means we are called to be the person God wants us to be. We are called to follow the path God has laid out for us, a path that will accomplish His Will and lead us to Him. We are called to be our own unique branch and remain attached to our source, who supports us and gives us everything we need to grow and thrive.

We find the strength we need when we stop fighting God and gracefully accept His will for us. When we trust that He knows better. When we stop looking at others and the different gifts God has given them, and start developing and being grateful for the ones He has given us.

It doesn't matter how big our glass is, it only matters that it is full. We have a purpose, one that is tied directly to Christ Jesus, The Vine, and as long as we stay connected to Him, we will not wither away.

God blesses the weary. It may not be a visible blessing for all to see but within us God grants very special graces that have the power to refresh and transform. Over time, these graces will show in every area of our lives. It is in these unseen blessings that we become strong.

"I ask God from the wealth of his glory to give you power through His Spirit to be strong in your inner selves, and I pray that Christ will make His home in your hearts through faith" (Eph 3:16-17) It is through the power of The Holy Spirit that we are renewed each day. The Spirit breathes new life into us and through this holy breath we are free and flexible and strong in Christ Jesus The Lord.

The Holy Spirit is our help. We can call upon God The Holy Spirit every single day of our lives in prayer, asking Him to strengthen our hearts, minds, souls and bodies and to give us the power of God for our day.

Let's not be deceived. There is only one Holy Spirit. He is God Himself, the third person of The Most Blessed Trinity and He infuses us with His Divine Love, washing us clean, making us new and calm, light and clear, refreshed and ready. The Spirit of Christ has the power to make us strong! Let's remain in Him. Let's be open to His healing touch in our lives, and draw strength from His unconditional Love.

When we allow our lives to be directed by The Holy Spirit, we give Him permission to not only guide us, but to also grace us with every blessing that we need to accomplish His purpose.

Without God we can do nothing. But we are not without God. *"For in Him we live and move and have our being"* (Acts 17:28).

Prayer

Dear Lord, you are the vine and the source from which all graces flow. I ask to receive these graces and the joy you promise to your followers. I pray that I will stay connected to you at all times.

Lord, I know that there is a purpose for my struggles and while I may not understand it I ask for the grace to remain faithful and united to you no matter what. Apart from you there is no life. Help me to appreciate my place in your plan and to carry out your will for my life joyfully. I am completely dependent upon you for this joy and I ask to receive it now.

Please pour out your Holy Spirit upon me and everyone near and dear to me, and refresh our tired souls. Make us new in heart, mind, body and spirit. Clear the path for us to walk with confidence in You. In Jesus name. Amen.

New Way Today

-

3

"Wait for the Lord, be strong and take heart, and wait for the Lord."

(Psalm 27:14)

God's timing is perfect. Our timing isn't. We trust God with our plans, we know He will come through, but it's taking way longer than we thought it would. We think we've been patient long enough and now our patience is wearing thin.

Maybe we start off with a great new idea or feel enthusiastic about a project. Maybe we're confident that a new door is about to open in our lives in some way or that a situation we are praying over will turn around. But then our prayer loses its enthusiasm and we start to doubt. We wonder if maybe we were mistaken, if maybe we should move on to something else. Perhaps the whole thing should be scratched because if it were God's will it would have happened already.

No doubt there are instances when this is certainly true, where things are going nowhere because they're not supposed to. Maybe it's not God's plan for us or maybe He has something different, and better, in store. We need to continue to pray over situations like these to make sure it is truly God guiding us.

But sometimes, we are tempted to abandon our prayer too quickly because it's taking too long or not going the way we think it should. Sometimes we get tired of "waiting on the Lord" and it is exactly during these times that our Lord tells us to continue to wait on Him, with faith. If you notice in this chapter's scripture, *"wait for the Lord"* is said twice in one sentence, encouraging us to be courageous and solid in our prayer.

"Rejoice in hope, endure in affliction, persevere in prayer" (Rom 12:12). Prayer itself is strength for our souls. God is with us at every moment but He is present with us in a very particular way when we pray, when we reach out to Him. Prayer is where we find grace. We draw upon the strength of God through this connection we have to Him in our hearts in prayer. Therefore, it is very important to make time for prayer each day and remain faithful to it.

We can pray for discernment, the grace to know what God wants us to do in a particular situation. We can pray for wisdom and ask God to reveal His plan for us at this time in our lives. We can pray for the grace to trust God's perfect timing like never before. We can ask God to dispel doubts and confirm our prayer, or even to put a new desire in our hearts. Above all, let's pray to persevere in prayer when we least feel like it, knowing that God is building us up and making us strong, no matter what the outcome.

"We are afflicted in every way, but not constrained; perplexed, but not driven to despair; persecuted, but not abandoned, struck down, but not destroyed." (2Cor 4:8-9). Let's pray for faith in the victory Christ won on the cross, knowing we too will not be defeated.

Waiting for the Lord doesn't have to be passive. We can be active during this time in faith and charity, being a blessing to others, even when things aren't going our way. We can resist the temptation to get down and discouraged by allowing the Light of Christ to shine through us despite our difficulties.

Let's pray to be a light in someone else's life who is also struggling. Even in the midst of our own affliction we can still grow in holiness for "affliction produces endurance, and endurance, proven character, hope, and hope does not disappoint, because the love of God has been poured out into our hearts through The Holy Spirit that has been given to us" (Rom 5: 3-5).

Prayer

Dear Lord, only you know what this situation means to me. You know how long I have prayed and waited but I wish to give you this prayer again. This time with more confidence and trust in your all-knowing wisdom of what is best for me. You know what will truly make me happy.

Please fill my heart with new enthusiasm, energy and inspiration. Please even fill my heart with a new prayer if you would like me to let go of the old one. Help me to see that the greatest prayer I can ask for is to be who you want me to be, and do what you want me to do. Please open my eyes and my heart to your wisdom, so that I may experience your joy even now. Please guide me what to pursue and what to abandon. Help me to see what is truly your will.

Lord, help me to persevere in the hope you have placed before me. Help me to truly seek your desire in the outcome of this situation, for I trust that your way is the right one. Lord, please pour out your grace upon me and give me strength and peace over this. In Jesus name. Amen.

4

"The Lord is my strength and my shield.

My heart trusts in Him, and He helps me."

(Psalm 28:7)

Our hearts can't handle it all. Our strength is not enough. Much of our suffering comes from relying on our own strength to carry us through life. But God is our strength and He promises to be our shield. He will guard and protect our hearts from bearing too heavy a burden.

We experience His strength the most, when we trust in Him. We are to place our trust in who He is, not in what He can do for us. We Trust God, because He's God. He knows what's best. He loves us and wants us to have peace of soul, and He will bring about a good ending.

Our Lord loves us. He knows we're weak and imperfect, and He loves us just the same. He knows how much life can weigh us down – by hurt, pain, sin, guilt, fear, broken relationships, work, health problems, family responsibilities, lack of sleep, etc. You name it and God knows it. He knows that we need strength in each of these areas of our lives. But the strength we most need is strength for our souls when they are weary - when we've placed our hope in God, and still feel overwhelmed and about to break. This is when we are called to trust Him the most.

It is exactly when we are at our breaking point when it's most important to place everything at the foot of the cross and surrender to God, letting Him take over and do for us what we cannot do for ourselves. This might sound like giving up but really it's opening up the door to healing. It gives us a chance to start again.

By emptying ourselves of us, we can be filled with Christ. We are weak and limited, but God isn't. Sometimes just admitting we need help is the real battle, but that simple act of acknowledging our need for God can set us free. We want to be able to handle everything ourselves. But we weren't made for that. We were made for God.

God wants to protect our hearts from discouragement and give us hope. He can change our lives, and we can become refreshed and empowered. We will receive *"a new heart and a new spirit"* (Ez 36:26) just as He promised. When we trust in God's power to help us, He will.

"In all these things we conquer overwhelmingly through Him who loved us. For I am convinced that neither death, nor life, nor angels, nor principalities, nor present things, nor future things, nor powers, nor height, nor depth, nor any other creature will be able to separate us from the love of God in Christ Jesus our Lord." (Romans 8:37-39)

The power of God's Love will sustain us. We receive this power when we humbly admit we are in need of it. Our Lord will never abandon us. This too really shall pass. A new day is coming. There is light at the end of this tunnel, and God will help us get there.

Prayer

Dear Lord, you've seen what I can do with my own power. You see where it's gotten me. My own strength is not enough. I need you. I need your help. I need you to carry me, sometimes like a little child who's so tired they can't even take another step. I need you to lift me up and hold me. Please help me to stop seeing my need for you as a sign of weakness. Help me not to be ashamed or too proud to admit that I need you. Help me to accept the help you offer to me. Please breathe new life into me and make all things new. In Jesus name, Amen.

New Way Today

5

"Cast all your anxiety on Him because He cares for you."

(1 Peter 5:7)

At times it can feel as though the weight of the world is on our backs. How wonderful it would be to free ourselves of this heavy burden. Wouldn't it be nice to let go of fear and worry?

This hardly seems realistic though, since we have so much to worry about. It almost feels unnatural not to be anxious about things. But we have a God who tells us that we can cast our cares on Him, and through Jesus, have a new reality.

Jesus died to give us new life, one that is free from fear. This is a grace we receive through prayer. On our own, it's not possible. But we're not on our own. God is with us. He's never left us and He never will.

When we pray for the grace to see our lives in the light of Christ, things will become clearer. We will see that we have a loving God protecting us. We will begin to see what a useless, non-productive emotion worry is. We will begin to see that fear holds us back from becoming the people God wants us to be, and this is why it is so important that we overcome it.

It may sound simplistic, but in this scripture we hear that we can cast our cares on God because He cares for us. It is in His arms that we are safe. It is through His Love, that we are sheltered. It is because of His heart, that we can live freely. God really does care about every single one of His children and all of their needs. He knows our struggles and what burdens us the most. He knows us better than we do.

Most of all, God knows what will free us from fear and anxiety. He knows the unique, personal graces that we need. He's ready to pour them out upon us. Let's be ready to receive them.

"Therefore do not worry about tomorrow, for tomorrow will worry about itself. Each day has enough trouble of its own" (Mt 6:34). We can make a decision to practice prayer daily and to grow in our relationship with Jesus. As we do, we will slowly learn better ways to cope with the natural inclination to worry and instead trust in His divine providence to take care of us.

Let's not look too closely at our own weaknesses but keep our eyes fixed on Christ so that we won't get discouraged. We have a good and loving God, who's in control. He has our life in the palm of His hand, and He won't let us go.

Prayer

Dear Lord, I don't want fear to control my life anymore. I want you to. I don't want worry to guide my steps. I want you to. I don't want anxiety to occupy my thoughts. I want you to. Help me Jesus, to grow in my relationship with you and as a result of growing in Love, fear will flee, because "perfect love casts out fear."

Please give me the freedom of being a child of God filled with faith and trusting in my Heavenly Father to take care of all of my needs. Please give my mind a rest. Please give my heart a rest. Please give me the peace you died to give me. Please bless my family and take care of all of their needs and free them from fear as well.

Lord, please grant me the grace to Trust you more and more, and I know that over time, worry will become less and less. You are the answer. Help me to keep praying to be set free from my fears, for I know this is your will for me for you have said, "Be not afraid." I humbly ask for this grace now. I thank you and I love you. In Jesus name. Amen.

New Way Today

6

"I can do all things through Him who strengthens me."

(Philippians 4:13)

Through Him. Not through our own effort. But through Jesus, who's strength never runs out.

When we depend on only our own strength we will become overwhelmed and discouraged. But Jesus has the power to lift our burden or give us the grace to carry it. He carries it with us and carries us through it. He is our source of strength, inside and out.

It is Jesus who gives us the strength to keep going. Even at the brink of exhaustion, we can turn to the Lord and be refreshed. But too often we wait until we are exhausted before we turn to Him. We try to do things on our own merit, sometimes taking on too much, and quickly become overwhelmed.

Other times, we are just worn out from the responsibilities we have toward family, work, friends and community. After a long day of physical and emotional struggle, simply going shopping at the grocery store can be a chore and a challenge. But God is so good, and will help us with even that. He wants to come with us. He wants to be everywhere we are.

God wants us to turn to Him in *"all things"* even the most routine. God is not limited. We can never exhaust His strength. It's endless, and available to us now. He will give us the energy to keep going when things get tough.

Whether it's physical, emotional, mental, spiritual, family, work, school, or relationship struggles, God can handle it. Even when we are just plain tired, God hears our prayer and wants us to open our hearts to Him and be renewed.

I'm sure we've already prayed about our concerns and perhaps we're frustrated that we're not seeing results, and still feel worn out and discouraged. We were hoping by now, that our burden would be lighter already.

Suffering is a mystery, but God does truly give us the grace to sustain it and gives us His peace during trials. There may be many unseen reasons why it is going on so long but God sees the whole picture, we only see part. He may be helping others during this time of suffering, who have prayers similar to ours but we practice patience because *"we know that all things work for good for those who love God, who are called according to His purpose"* (Rom 8:28).

In the meantime let's allow God to carry us through it in the arms of His love, confident that He really is working all things out for our good. Let's look at Jesus on the cross, and unite our suffering to His, knowing that what looks like a defeat is a victory in disguise. Our Lord took on these same burdens and emotions. Let's trust Him with ours.

"I consider that the sufferings of this present time are as nothing compared with the glory to be revealed for us" (Rom 8:18). We all have crosses to carry in life. Some are much bigger than others, but we are all called to unite our cross to the Cross of Christ.

Through Christ, who will provide us the grace and strength we need, we can do God's will. We can carry out God's work and fulfill His plans, and in doing so He will provide all that we need to complete the tasks He has entrusted us with. He gives us both the job *and* the tools we need to accomplish it. This is what "*through Him*" means. We can do all that God wants us to do.

When we invite Jesus into our struggle, He comes, and grace flows. Grace is a difficult thing to explain but you will know it when you experience it. It can happen from one moment to the next. One minute we may feel like despairing, and after praying we suddenly feel refreshed and energized again. We receive grace. It's a gift. When we pray, we must be open to grace entering in. We must let go of pride and humbly admit we can't do it on our own. We need our God.

It's important to continually evaluate our prayer intentions to see if they are God-centered. We are called to pray with faith. It's not easy to keep a positive attitude all the time but our general mindset should be one of believing that things will get better and God will make a way. We must have hope in order to activate faith.

We should be less concerned with defining exactly what the answer to our prayer will look like, and more concerned with believing that whatever the answer is will be the right one. Let's give God room to surprise us, and find our peace in knowing He will make the best situation work out for us. As long as it comes from God, we will have the right answer.

We can count on God's help every day. He will help us in even the smallest things. But without His grace supporting us, these small things soon pile up and become a big thing. So let's ask Jesus to help us with everything.

We can rely on God. When we fully accept that God is good, loving and that He has a perfect plan in store for us, it will be easier to rely on His strength. When we truly believe that He cares about every single detail of our lives, we can learn to trust Him more and more. When we actually desire what He wants, He will supply the strength and the rest we need, at the right time, in the right way, every day.

Prayer

Dear Lord, only you know my heart. Only you know how I really feel. Help me to be open and honest with you in prayer. Lord, I feel wiped out. I feel like I am at a stop sign and I can't go any further. I'm getting discouraged and I know this isn't your will for me, but I'm starting to lose hope. I need you to step in.

Day after day, I am struggling. I humbly admit to you now that I can't handle my life on my own. I admit now, that I need you. The world tells me I can do anything I want if I put my mind to it, but my soul knows I can't do a thing without your grace to support me. Please pour out upon me that perfect combination of receiving your grace and acting upon it. Help me to keep my eyes on you when I feel I'm sinking. Help me to keep moving forward. Help me to do the work that you want me to do, trusting you will provide all that I need.

Lord, I thank you for carrying me through everything you have so far. I can't even imagine the unseen blessings I have received. Please continue to grace me with your strength. Teach me what it means to rely on you. Teach me what it means to draw my strength from yours.

I love you Lord, and I'm trying my best. When my best doesn't feel like it's enough, hold me, heal me and help me. Strengthen me, my Lord and my God. In Jesus name. Amen.

7

"Those who sow with tears

will reap with songs of joy!"

(Psalm 126:5)

The Cross. What does it mean to us? When we look at Jesus on a crucifix, what thoughts come to mind? Do we see a victory or a defeat? Do we see the beginning or the end? Do we see life or do we see death?

"The Lord is close to the brokenhearted, and saves those who are crushed in spirit" (Ps 34:18). Christ gives us an example to follow when we endure pain, sorrow and confusion. Jesus taught us to trust our heavenly Father in all circumstances. He taught us not to judge by the world's opinions of success or failure, but to do what God calls us to do and leave the results in His hands. Jesus showed us a love that is eternal, even in the midst of unspeakable suffering.

Jesus understands our humanity. He knows where our tears come from, and how long they've been there. He knows our disappointments, our brokenness, and our fears. God became a human being in the person of Jesus Christ. Jesus is truly God and truly man. He understands our emotions and came to heal our hearts.

When we are going through a trial, we might get frustrated hearing that everything will be ok, that things will work out for the best, or that God will open another door. While all of these are true, they are not always a comfort in the moment.

No one could ever truly understand our pain other than God. Our loved ones may mean well, and should try their best to love and support us, but they're not God and we shouldn't expect them to be. Even if no one notices, we should not harvest any anger. They are fighting their own battles and have their own secret tears that only God knows about. Our emotional struggles take place in the silence of our hearts and this is where the Lord is. He sees, and understands.

But we are told in this scripture that our tears will end, and that we will rejoice. We are called to believe this by faith. Through prayer, God will provide us the grace we need to hold on, to trust in Him, and to receive His peace during even the worst trials in life. *"For everything there is a season, and a time for every matter under heaven"* (Eccles 3:1).

Emotions are tricky and can deceive us. We may feel like things will never get better. When we are in pain, it may feel like we will always be in pain. This is a lie and does not come from God. When we stand on the word of God and proclaim, even through the tears, that He will deliver us from this difficult time, we open up the floodgates of God's grace to work in our lives.

It's very difficult to speak encouraging words and proclaim good things to come when we're feeling down, but turning to the word of God is the very best thing we can do in these situations. It is *The Spirit that gives life.* *"The words I have spoken to you—they are full of the Spirit and life"* (John 6:63).

Jesus has given us the words needed to lift our spirit. We hear His voice in scripture. When we are feeling defeated, it's the perfect time to open the Bible or pray. These are the weapons that will turn our situation around, and by God's grace working through His word, and through prayer, our tears will turn into rejoicing. God has promised it, and He will do it.

Jesus loves us. He knows what's going on in our lives. He isn't ignoring our situation, and the only thing God forgets is our sins. He remembers every prayer we've ever said, every hope we've ever had, and every tear we have ever cried. He is holding us now, loving us now, inviting us now to take His hand and allow Him to show us another way, the way of real peace, the way that leads to Him.

God has promised that *"He will wipe every tear from their eyes. There will be no more death or mourning or crying or pain, for the old order of things has passed away."* *(Rev 21:4)* He has promised that He will make *"everything new!"* (Rev 21:5)

The cross is a victory. It brings about a new beginning. It puts to death all that needs to be put to death and brings to life all that needs to be brought to life. We worship a living God, Christ Jesus, raised from the dead, who has overcome all obstacles. His suffering was tremendous but through the tears of Jesus, our wounds can be healed. Through His wounds, our tears can be washed away. We can rise with Him.

Let's intensify our prayer life by being more dedicated to it and more open to God when we pray. Let's give Him a chance to show Himself to us in a new way. Let's unite our tears to His, firm in the belief that there is a victory in here somewhere and The Lord will bring us to it.

Let's pray for the grace to be willing to believe this. Let's ask Jesus, honestly in prayer to heal our hearts, however He wants to. Let's give God permission to make us new, to bring us to a place where we will one day rejoice forever.

In the meanwhile we walk with confidence knowing that He walks with us. Every single day Christ is by our side. Peace will soon override the pain, and hope will override our tears. The weary will be set free and God will put a new desire in our hearts. Life will be good again.

There really is a reason you are going through all of this. It might not make sense now, but God has a good and holy purpose for your life, and all the people in it. God has not abandoned you. Your suffering is holy and it will bring you to a better place. God can put the pieces back together, in a way that will set us free.

Prayer

Dear Lord, only you understand the tears I cry. Only you know the real reasons I cry them. Only you Jesus have the power to heal me and bring my heart into a new place, one that is lighter and brighter than what I feel now.

Grant me the gift of faith in times of trial, believing that you have not abandoned me. Grant me the grace to not abandon you, but to trust in your infinite Goodness, in all circumstances, even and especially the ones that make no sense to me. When I feel like despairing help me to contemplate your Holy Cross, and see you yourself trusting The Father in all things, even in death.

Help me to remember that things are not always what they seem. Your Cross looks like the end, but it's really the beginning. Your Cross looks like a defeat, but it's really a victory. Your Cross looks hopeless, but from it comes eternal life. Help me in my struggles to always remember the Joy of the Resurrection, and the newness you can bring to my life even now.

Lord, I look forward to the day when you will wipe away every tear from my eyes and make all things new. Please strengthen my weary soul. Increase my faith in you. Help me to be an example of your unfailing Love to others. Come Lord Jesus, when my prayer fails me and I can't find the words, just come Lord Jesus into my heart, and make me whole. Amen.

8

"Do not be afraid; do not be discouraged,

for the Lord your God will be with you

wherever you go."

(Joshua 1:9)

You're never alone. God The Father doesn't leave His children, not even for a second.

Our Lord walks with us. He supports us with His grace and guides us by His Spirit. He knows what direction we're heading in, and whether it's the right one. He can help us change course if need be, and will love us through it.

Our Lord tells us in this scripture that He is always with us, at all times and in all places. He is with us *wherever* we go. He never leaves us to figure things out on our own. He is always available to guide us when we seek His help.

God meets us where we are, and guides us to where we should be. You are here. This is the starting point. Whatever the past, God will meet us in the present. We don't have to get it together first. We must turn to God first, then we will get it together.

We need to let go of perfect. We have to let go of spiritual pride and accept our human limitations and weaknesses. We don't have to be "right" or a certain way before we let God into our lives. Again, it is when we allow God into our lives that things will be put right. *"But seek first his kingdom and his righteousness, and all these things will be given to you as well" (Matt 6:33).*

God is faithful. He is Good. He never leaves. His Love is unconditional, and always available to us. It is by His grace that fear and discouragement will flee from our lives and a newfound peace will arrive.

So let's pray more intently for the grace to have confidence in God's presence in our lives, especially when we feel afraid or discouraged. Let's draw strength from His presence in our lives by being more open to His will for us. Let's remember that Jesus endured all these hardships Himself, and He died to give us a new life.

Prayer

Dear Lord, I know you are with me wherever I go. I want the abundant life you died to give me. I really do want to be open to your plan for my life and to trust you with everything, but I'm human and weak and need your help. I'm a sinner in need of your mercy and grace. I'm so glad you are always ready to lift me up and carry me through. Thank you for loving me just the way I am.

I give to you now the present moment. This is where I am at this time in my life. I give you my situation just as it is. Lord I surrender to you my current path. I lift up my past and its regrets to you for healing, and pray for the grace to learn from it and begin again. Help me to truly surrender everything about me to you. Help me to be yours. In thought, word and deed please help me to be more like you.

Please inspire me with a new dream, a new hope, a new idea. Help me to forgive what needs forgiving. Help me to love and forgive myself also. Above all, please fill me with the knowledge that you are always with me. Wherever I go, you are at home in my heart. Help me to draw strength from your presence within and grant me the gift of faith at all times. Please fill my heart with your love and there will be no more room for fear or doubt. In Jesus' name. Amen.

9

"I have told you these things, so that in me you
may have peace. In this world you will have
trouble. But take heart! I have overcome the
world."

John 16:33

Sometimes the weight of the world feels like it's on our shoulders. Our own strength fails us. We need a Savior.

In the person of Jesus Christ we find one. The only one who can give us true peace. Our Lord tells us here not to be surprised when trouble comes, when life is hard. He especially makes it a point in the gospels to tell us it will be hard to be His follower at times. The world rejected Christ, and may reject us too, and as strange as this might sound – it's ok.

Our goal as Christians is not to fit in with the world, our goal is to follow Christ. To do what God wants us to do, and be who God wants us to be.

When we suffer, we are actually in good company. Jesus suffered too, and He overcame it.

By His grace, so will we. Jesus has elevated suffering into something that God can use, something holy that will bring us closer to Him. We will grow in holiness and come out of it stronger than before.

Jesus has the victory. It is through Him only that we experience true victory in our own lives as well. At times when we are weary, our Lord invites us to recall His words. The gospel is for all people. He is not just speaking to those who heard His voice over two thousand years ago. He's talking to you, now.

"Peace I leave with you; my peace I give you" (John 14:27). In this very moment Jesus is gently trying to draw us closer to Himself. He wants to set us free from the heaviness in our hearts. When things seem dull Jesus can turn on His Light in our souls and refresh us, making us new and alive again! But He won't force Himself into our lives. He needs our consent.

The victory our Lord has won on the Cross is a victory that occurs within our souls. The world may not see it or understand, but we are all created for eternity and are called to grow in holiness. It is this spiritual growth that defeats discouragement as we permit the grace of Christ to transform our lives.

This grace is available to us at all times, but especially when we are going through something difficult. We don't always look for God's grace when things are going well, but we do when our strength fails us. We look to Heaven for help, and when we do, the Kingdom of God within us will respond.

Help is available. *"He who is in you is greater than he who is in the world"* (1 John 4:4). Our circumstances may not change right away, but *we* can change. Right now we can begin to pray, to make better decisions personally and spiritually. We can change our attitude about things, and decide how we want to spend this time of our lives. What sort of person do we want to be on the inside? Do we want to reflect Christ to others as we go through this trial?

Finally, we can't ignore in this scripture our Lord's desire to give us peace. He says, *"in Me"* you may have peace. Do we look for peace and fulfillment in Jesus? Or do we look to people, places and things to fill our soul?

As we grow in faith by prayer, our lives will change. Things will get better. Let's be willing to change our definition of what that means, and allow God, who knows what He's doing, make things better for us His way, and in His perfect time.

Prayer

Dear Lord, in the world I have trouble, just as you said. In the world, I don't see you as I wish I did. In the world, you are forgotten and as your follower I too feel the pain of those who reject you. You have told me this is to be expected, and I know I shouldn't be surprised when trouble comes, but I ask you to have mercy on me. At times, I feel weak and tired and I can't overcome these troubles on my own. I need your help and your grace working in my life.

Lord, help me to tap into that special place within me that is undisturbed in time of trouble. That special place where everything is ok. Help me to find my comfort and my joy in your presence within me, and not depend on what is happening around me. Help me not to look to the world for the victory and peace that I long for, but instead look to you, who alone holds power over the world.

Dear Jesus, no matter what the world throws at me you are at my side. Please give me the gift of faith to believe in your presence in my life. Help me to realize you could not possibly

54

abandon us and if you permit me to undergo a trial, then good will come from it, for you are Goodness itself.

Lord Jesus, I know you love me. You loved me to death, and you love me still. I pray for the grace to trust in this Love you have for me. You would not suffer the way you did and then forget about me. I know you are here. Please reveal yourself to me in a new way and refresh me. Jesus, Prince of Peace, come into my heart and the hearts of everyone near and dear to me, and give us the confidence, hope and strength that we need for this day. Amen.

New Way Today

10

"Therefore encourage one another and build each other up, just as in fact you are doing."

1 Thessalonians 5:11

We are always called to love our neighbor, even when we might be going through a hard time. When things are not going our way, it's easy to forget that other people have problems in their lives too. We're not the only ones who are weary or burdened.

God is kind and merciful and He knows our struggles and how they impact our lives. It's natural that our own feelings will take priority over other people's, and God understands how our current situation affects us.

Yet He still expects us to be an example of His love to others, even, and maybe especially, during times of trial. There is no greater witness than for all to see that we trust the Lord in good times, and bad.

Even our words can have a big impact in somebody else's life. Regardless of how we feel, we can always choose what we say (or don't say).

We can lift somebody up or tear them down. We are called in this scripture to *encourage one another and build each other up*, despite our circumstances. We can simply recognize that while we may be in turmoil, others may be also.

Every person has their own cross to carry in life, and maybe we can help. Everyone gets weary at times and we can bring the love of Jesus to them and help them carry their load too.

It may be the very last thing we feel like doing, but ironically such an act delivers us from our own discouragement. It brings us out of ourselves and activates love within us. It puts God in motion.

We can be the encouraging person that someone doesn't have in their lives. We can be that listening ear or kind word they wouldn't have heard otherwise. We can be the hug they wouldn't have gotten. We can pray for them.

The Lord can use us, at all times, and in many ways. We can encourage others to trust in God, and provide them hope, just as we need hope and encouragement for ourselves.

"For as in one body we have many parts, and all the parts do not have the same function, so we, though many, are one body in Christ and

individually parts of one another" (Rom 12:4-5). We are one body in Christ. When one of our members hurt, we can come to their aid and bring healing.

"Give, and it will be given to you" (Luke 6:38). It's when we give that we receive, so let's not forget our neighbor even in the midst of our own weariness. We can pray for their situation and take the time to recognize their needs. We can put them first and The Holy Spirit will bless us too.

Each one of us is called to *"encourage the disheartened, help the weak, be patient with everyone. Make sure that nobody pays back wrong for wrong, but always strive to do what is good for each other and for everyone else. Rejoice always, pray continually, give thanks in all circumstances, for this is God's will for you in Christ Jesus.* (1 Thes 5:14-18)

God is with you. He hears your prayers, and He sees your tears. He knows your struggles, disappointments, and frustration. He knows how long it's taking, and how much you've hoped. He is not indifferent to your pain, or anybody else's.

Let's be the light that we wish others would be to us. Let's lift our hearts to God and pray for the grace to love our neighbor as He has loved us. Let's keep our eyes fixed on Christ Jesus, to seek first the Kingdom of God, the Kingdom of Love, and our situation will fall into place. By putting Jesus first, by loving our neighbor as He has commanded, we will find strength for ourselves.

Prayer

Dear Lord, I find it hard to help others when I am in need of help myself. I honestly don't think of their struggles as I should, because my own problems overwhelm me.

I'm just having a tough time Lord, and I wish you would help me. I need you. At the same time, help me to see that others need you too and that I can be an instrument of grace that you can use to help them.

Help me to see that the way you pour out your love is through us. Help me to bring your love to others and be an example of a Christian who trusts their Savior. Help me to build others up, to help lighten their burden through action and prayer.

Help me to speak words of life and encouragement. I know that you are with me Lord and that I will come out of this trial better than before. Help me to do your will always, even in the midst of my own pain. Lord, please bring healing to me and everyone that I help. Give me a new way, one that brings peace to me and everyone around me. In Jesus' name. Amen.

Conclusion

LETS NOT WEARY OURSELVES

We're doing the best we can, with what we have, at this time. Let's not get down on ourselves. Let's give ourselves some credit. Our Lord loves us just the way we are and He doesn't expect us to carry our burden alone. He wants to carry it for us. Our Lord doesn't expect us to find our own strength when we are weary. He wants us to find His.

He doesn't tell us our suffering has no meaning, He says "*Blessed are you*." He doesn't want us to try and make a way, He says, *"I Am The Way."* He doesn't tell us to lift ourselves up and get it together. He says, "*Come to Me.*"

God knows the strength we need comes from Him alone. No one else can give it to us. The world and its empty promises will leave us feeling deserted and abandoned by God, when it was never capable of giving us what we needed anyway. People are not God and they can't fill our souls. There is a place within each one of us that was created by our Creator, that only our Creator can fill. We belong to Him. We come from Him, and everything we need comes from Him.

Our Strength is from the Lord. We can look for it elsewhere, but we'll be back looking for God again soon enough. Jesus wants to spare us further pain and invites us to accept His invitation now. He invites us to look to Him so that our burden will become light. He invites us to receive His peace, a peace the world can't give us. Jesus invites us to place our trust in Him. Without trust we are just closing our eyes and hoping for the best.

Faith is confidence in God. We are sure of His presence in our lives, whether we feel Him there or not. We know He will come through for us. No matter what shape it takes, we believe everything will turn out right.

God has not abandoned us, and He never will. We can expect to live the abundant spiritual life Jesus died to give us, because He has told us that's why He came. *"I have come that they may have life, and have it to the full"* (John 10:10).

Everything happens for a reason, and your current struggle is perhaps part of your path to holiness. There are many reasons we may become burdened. Some are in our control and can be changed and others are trials we just have to walk through. There's no way around them. But either way, we don't walk alone.

Things will get better. God has a plan and it includes a lighter and brighter future. It may not feel like it now, and that's understandable, but life is constantly changing and as we grow in faith and further develop our relationship with The Lord we will change too.

It won't be this way forever, and we shouldn't despair in the meantime because our Lord says "*My grace is sufficient for you, for my power is made perfect in weakness*" (2 Cor 12:9). God will provide us what we need at every step, and hold our hand along the way. Let's make an act of faith and lean on Him.

With so much out there that can bring us down, let's not add ourselves to the list. There's enough that can weary and burden us, let's make a conscience effort not to weary ourselves too. Let's be mindful of how we think of ourselves and speak about ourselves. We are each a child of God, a member of the body of Christ, and the Holy Spirit dwells within us - and no one can take that away. We have eternal value.

Let's make a renewed daily effort to turn to prayer and scripture, and choose the words we use, so that we speak words of life and encouragement. Let's let go of perfect. It doesn't exist anyway.

Let's give ourselves permission to make mistakes without self-condemnation.

We all have our moments when things feel overwhelming, like we can't take another step, or we feel there's no point anymore. This is exactly when we can call upon the Lord with confidence to receive His grace. *"'Even now,' declares the Lord, 'return to me with all your heart'"* (Joel 2:12).

These are moments of surrender. These are the moments we need to praise God, even if we don't feel like it. These are the moments we need to be active, even when we don't feel like it. These are the moments we need to pray and trust and be thankful for what we have, even when we don't feel like it. These are the moments we need to seek a helping hand and lend one to others in need.

Sometimes we are harder on ourselves than anyone else, and we make life all the more harder by comparing ourselves with others. Let's take a moment to acknowledge our own individual worth and value as a child of God, loved unconditionally by Him right now, just the way we are.

Let's recognize the steps we're taking to turn to God and grow in our faith, and be proud of ourselves for doing so. Even reading this book is a positive step that brings us closer to a new life. Striving towards personal and spiritual growth is an effort that should be commended. Not everyone attempts it, and you have, so be pleased with yourself. You are already moving forward!

Let's be at peace knowing God knows. Whether our struggle is obvious to others or hidden within, God sees and understands. Let's be people of forgiveness toward others and forgive ourselves for the past. Let's be kind and patient with ourselves during this difficult time.

As we open the door of our hearts to God's grace, *"rivers of living water will flow from within"* (John 7:38) and we will be made brand new. It is only through this fountain of life that we will find the healing and strength we need. Everything will be ok.

There really is rest for the weary. His name is Jesus. He promises to make our burden light. There is reason to hope! As we continue to pray, reflect on the cross, trust The Father, and love our neighbor as Christ has loved us, The Holy Spirit will move in our lives in a new way, and graces in times of trial will begin to overflow.

May God's Love bless you and strengthen you.

New Way Today

"May our Lord Jesus Christ himself and God our Father, who loved us and by His grace gave us eternal encouragement and good hope, encourage your hearts and strengthen you in every good deed and word." (2 Thess 2:16-17)

GOD IS GOOD, ALL THE TIME.

ALL THE TIME, GOD IS GOOD.

New Way Today

Site Information

Join us online for more inspirational scripture
reflections and prayers.

Website:
http://www.newwaytoday.net

Social Media:
www.instagram.com/newwaytoday1
www.pinterest.com/NewWayToday

New Way Today Books

*A New You! Letting Go of the Past, Trusting God with our
Future.*

Strength For The Weary, Finding Grace in Times of Trial.

Prayers For A New Way. A Prayer Book for the Heart.

New Way Today Inspirational Reflections For The Soul.

Silent Prayer: Be Still and Know That I Am God.

*The Truth of God's Love, In Ten Words or Less:
Affirmations of Faith.*

Visit New Way Today's Amazon Book Page for more.

May God Bless you, and everyone near and dear to you.

New Way Today

Made in United States
Troutdale, OR
03/29/2024